DRUG DANGERS

MARIJUANA
DRUG DANGERS

Gary L. Somdahl

Enslow Publishers, Inc.

40 Industrial Road   PO Box 38
Box 398   Aldershot
Berkeley Heights, NJ 07922   Hants GU12 6BP
USA   UK

http://www.enslow.com

Dedicated to my wife and best friend, Cathleen

Library of Congress Cataloging-in-Publication Data

Somdahl, Gary L.
    Marijuana drug dangers / Gary L. Somdahl.
        p. cm. — (Drug dangers)
    Includes bibliographical references and index.
    Summary: Outlines the history, effects, and dangers of marijuana and how its abuse can be prevented and treated.
    ISBN 0-7660-1214-X
    1. Marijuana—Juvenile literature. 2. Marijuana—Psychological aspects—Juvenile literature. 3. Teenagers—Drug use—United States—Juvenile literature. [1. Marijuana. 2. Drug abuse.]
    I. Title. II. Series.
    HV5822.M3S65   1999
    362.29'5—dc21   98-51536
                                            CIP
                                            AC

Printed in the United States of America

10 9 8 7 6 5 4 3 2 1   JAN 2 4 2002

To Our Readers:
All Internet addresses in this book were active and appropriate when we went to press. Any comments can be sent by e-mail to Comments@enslow.com or to the address on the back cover.

Photo Credits: Corbis Digital Stock, p. 22; Copyright 1997, 1996 T/Maker Company, p. 15; Corel Corporation, pp. 7, 8, 17, 19, 27, 39, 40, 45; Díamar Interactive Corp., p. 53; Enslow Publishers, Inc., p. 20; ; National Archives, pp. 10, 13, 31, 33, 37, 49.

Cover Photo: National Archives

contents

Titles in the **Drug Dangers** series:

Alcohol Drug Dangers
ISBN 0-7660-1159-3

Crack and Cocaine Drug Dangers
ISBN 0-7660-1155-0

Diet Pill Drug Dangers
ISBN 0-7660-1158-5

Heroin Drug Dangers
ISBN 0-7660-1156-9

Inhalant Drug Dangers
ISBN 0-7660-1153-4

Marijuana Drug Dangers
ISBN 0-7660-1214-X

Speed and Methamphetamine Drug Dangers
ISBN 0-7660-1157-7

Steroid Drug Dangers
ISBN 0-7660-1154-2

one

Shannon's Story

Eleven-year-old Shannon (not her real name) stood in silence. She watched as the pipe passed from one person to the next. The awkward-looking gadget was filled to the brim with marijuana. Each of her friends slowly brought it to their lips, inhaled, and blew the harsh-smelling yellow smoke high into the air. It was her turn now.

Shannon became nervous when the pipe was passed to her. She stared down at the burning bowl. She hesitated and trembled slightly with worry. Her first thought was to walk away. She had always been taught by her parents and teachers that that was the right thing to do. She never expected to be around marijuana—until now. It was a surprise. She had heard stories of adults and older kids smoking it, but never kids her age. All she did was join some new friends behind the school after lunch for a little laughter, fun, and talk.

Before she knew what was happening, someone pulled out the pipe and lit it.

At first she recoiled in fear. She was speechless. This was not supposed to happen. Her head was spinning. She was thinking about how to gracefully leave without losing these friends. It was uncomfortable. It was an awkward place to be.

She did not want to appear weird, wimpy, or weak. Shannon decided that one time probably would not hurt. And besides, she was curious. No one outside this small circle of friends would ever have to know. "Go ahead," she told herself "It's not as bad as you think. Besides, you can quit anytime you want."

She took a drag and closed her eyes. She imagined it was all a dream. The bitter taste tickled her throat and forced her to cough and gag, reminding her that she was wide awake. Feeling somewhat dizzy and out of place, she handed the pipe to the next girl in line. Shannon was high and scared at the same time.

Taking the pipe again, she inhaled deeply and became more at ease. She felt less scared about getting into trouble. The drug had altered her mind. It gave her a sense of security. She became relaxed and felt numb.

Over time she found herself smoking marijuana on a regular basis. Shannon's interest in school dimmed. She dropped out of her favorite sport, soccer, and hardly studied at all. Classes began to bore her. Her hobbies and interests no longer seemed fun. It was as if her energy, enthusiasm, and zest for excitement had vanished. Her lack of motivation drew the attention of her parents. She became hostile and angry whenever they brought it up or expressed their concerns. She told herself marijuana

Over time, and with continued marijuana use, the user will begin to lose interest in things that were once interesting and exciting—such as sports and school.

was a way to cope with her feelings of frustration at not being able to get along with her parents.

Her friends had changed. The old ones kept far away. Those who had been with her since first grade were no longer there. Shannon hung out with many who had no regard for their future. They had little to do with their families. Most had been in trouble with the police. But she had one thing in common with them—smoking marijuana. The risks she came to take were more dangerous than ever before. There was the time she ran across a busy highway on a dare. Narrowly missing being run down by a pickup truck, Shannon laughed it off as no big deal. She even once stood on the railroad tracks, coming within inches of being hit by a fast-moving train. It was when she jumped off a deserted bridge over the Columbia River that her luck began to change.

She was carried downstream by waters that were swifter than she thought. She managed to hang on to a large boulder to which she had drifted. Several men in a boat rescued her. If they had not been there, she probably would have drowned. She was shaken up for a while, but it was soon forgotten. Shannon kept on using marijuana more and more frequently.

Her entire attitude and behavior changed. Shannon

Regular marijuana use can lead the user to risky behavior, without much regard for the consequences. Shannon's marijuana use resulted in her standing on the railroad tracks, coming within inches of being hit by a fast-moving train.

could not have cared less about her appearance. Her beautiful long blond hair lost its sparkle. Her bright blue eyes became tired and red. She looked dirty, unkempt, and uncared for. Her clothes were tattered and torn. Shannon was not the same happy girl who once had dreams of being the best. Her goals to finish school, attend college, and become a doctor had gone astray.

Shannon's thoughts turned toward getting high almost every day. It became her goal. It became her life. It occupied every moment of her waking hours. Skipping school and spending less time around her home became a habit. The constant fighting with her mother and father made her depressed. Shannon became filled with loneliness and desperation. She used to have a good relationship with them. Now she was uncertain whether she even loved herself.

Shannon became locked into the secret world of getting high. Little did she know she was trapped without knowing how to escape. She did not even realize she had a problem. Marijuana can be deceiving. It can come on as a best friend, but it can actually be an enemy. Those who smoke it are usually the last to know they have a problem.

Feeling confused, scared, and without hope, Shannon used the only tool she knew of to escape from having to deal with feelings of depression—marijuana. She was in a vicious circle that spiraled downward. She always reached for that same drug that had never let her down. Many times it had taken her away from reality to a land of make-believe. She believed it would make things easier, but it actually made them worse. Marijuana had made a huge impact on her life—one that would be felt for months to come.

It was only after being arrested for shoplifting that she began to see the mess she was in. Late one night she sat and thought about her life. What Shannon saw frightened her half to death. She had become a slave to marijuana. Somehow, before even realizing it, she had let it rule her head and her life. At first, she had taken the drug, and then the drug had taken her. And she had thought she could quit any time she wanted. Her mind raced as she realized she could have a problem. Shannon could find no way out. She did not know which way to turn. She had no idea what to do next.[1]

Those who use marijuana may feel that it helps them escape their problems. However, marijuana never makes problems disappear and can actually make them worse.

two

Marijuana and Society

Before the 1960s, many people had never heard of marijuana. Also known as pot, grass, weed, bud, and more than two hundred other names, it is the most often used illegal drug in America. It tends to be the first illegal drug young people use.[1] Its use among students in grades six through eight rose from 9.5 percent in 1994 to 14.7 percent in 1997. This is a 5.2 percent increase.[2] Though a 1998 survey showed a slight decline of 2.2 percent, the use of this often misunderstood drug continues to be a concern.

More than 2,251,000 people start using marijuana each year.[3] The chart on the following page shows the number of new users for this and other drugs for each year, month, week, day, hour, and minute.

Marijuana's popularity proves an important point. Many teens today do not consider it to be a

New Substance Users by Time Period

Substance	Year	Month	Week	Day	Hour	Minute
Nicotine	3,005,000	250,417	41,164	8,233	343	5.7
Alcohol	4,158,000	3,465,000	56,959	11,392	475	7.9
Heroin	122,000	10,167	1,671	334	14	0.2
Hallucinogens	912,000	76,000	12,493	2,499	104	1.7
Inhalants	666,000	55,500	9,123	1,825	76	1.3
Cocaine	533,000	44,417	7,301	1,460	61	1.0
Marijuana	2,251,000	187,583	30,836	6,167	257	4.3

Taken from the "Household Survey," Substance Abuse and Mental Health Services Administration, Advance Report No. 18, August 1996.

serious problem. The rate of those believing it is harmful has dropped drastically in the last few years. Many are ignoring the likelihood that marijuana could cause physical and emotional problems. While some claim it should be legalized, others believe it should only be used as medicine for cancer, AIDS, and glaucoma patients.

These claims may be due to the decrease of antidrug messages in the media and among the general population. It also could be due to an increase in prodrug messages in society. Many songs, movies, and television shows have glorified marijuana. It has also been made to appear safe and normal to use. T-shirts, caps, and posters with the picture of a marijuana leaf and a variety of captions are fast becoming a popular fad.

To change these messages, the Partnership for a

Drug-Free America began placing ads on television and in magazines. It was a serious attempt by the organization to prove that illegal drugs such as marijuana do more harm than good. One of the partnership's ads featured a picture of a marijuana plant with these words after it:

> *This is the weed that Jack bought. Jack got it from Bobby. Bobby is Jack's best friend. Bobby bought it from his pal at school, Tony. Tony knew this neighborhood connection—Sid or someone. Sid made a deal with a guy downtown who scored it from some dude down South who blew away two cops to get it over the border. Just for Jack.*

At the end of the story is a picture of two bullets with a bold headline that reads:

POT HOOKS YOU UP WITH A WHOLE NEW CIRCLE OF FRIENDS!

Marijuana use has been glorified in movies and on television. Despite this, it is still a mind-altering substance that causes problems for those who use it.

Another ad shows a girl with the barrel of a gun shoved up her nose. It's hard to forget those earlier commercials of an egg frying in a pan with a voice in the background saying, "This is your brain. . . . This is drugs. . . . This is your brain on drugs."

Unfortunately, these messages have kept few teens from experimenting with marijuana, alcohol, or other drugs. Many ignore the possibility that they could be taking a dangerous risk.

Parents and Guardians

Another reason for the climb in marijuana usage may be due to a misunderstanding and lack of honest information about it from parents. Some parents may even avoid the topic because they do not want to expose their own past drug use. Many mothers and fathers are unaware of the rise in drug use. Millions of parents believe that this threat to their children is a phase that will eventually go away. Others may not consider it an important issue at all.

In December 1994 Health and Human Services secretary Donna E. Shalala called for new enthusiasm in alerting the public, particularly parents, to the rising interest in drug use. Her message was loud and clear. She was concerned about marijuana's possible health consequences to young people. She called on parents to take action. Help was needed to prevent the return of a full-blown epidemic of teenage drug use. Many parents and teens have been slow to respond.

According to the Parent's Resource Institute for Drug Education (PRIDE), the percentage of young people who said their parents talk to them often about the dangers of marijuana and other drugs was lower than in past years.

Open and honest communication from parents and peers about the dangers of drug abuse may prevent someone from becoming a marijuana user.

A 1996 survey by PRIDE to determine who warns young people most about drugs showed that students learned more from teachers than they did from their parents. It also indicated that they learned even far less from friends.

Many parents of today's teens experimented with marijuana as students in college. This is often the reason they find it a difficult subject to talk about with their kids. As a result, they do not set strict ground rules against its use. And there are those who feel more comfortable waiting until their children are well into their late teens to discuss it. Today, however, marijuana use starts at a younger age. The average age of a first-time user is about thirteen and a half years old. Stronger forms of the drug

Who Warns Young People Most About Drugs

People who Warn	Percentage
Peers	11.7
Parents	29.6
Teachers	88.9

From PRIDE survey, 1996 (grades 6–12).

are available today than were years ago.[4] Research shows that the strength of marijuana has increased more than 275 percent over the past decade.[5] Recently, more data has been released. This new information suggests that smoking or eating marijuana baked into foods could have serious effects. It shows that the green or gray mixture of dried, shredded flowers and leaves of the cannabis plant could be harmful.

Effects of Marijuana

It is estimated that 35 to 50 million Americans have tried marijuana at least once. Between 12 and 18 million people are regular users of two or more joints (cigarettes) per week.[6] It is popular in many parts of the world, including the United States and Canada. Despite being against the law, many people continue to smoke it for its pleasurable and intoxicating effects. Though seen by many as "innocent fun," society as well as the users are sometimes the ones that suffer.

The symptoms and effects of marijuana depend

largely on the strength of the drug, how it is used, and what the user expects will happen. Some immediate reactions are feelings of relaxation, exhilaration, and intoxication. The heart rate increases slightly, pupils in the eye dilate, and there is some physical numbness. There usually is drowsiness and dizziness as well as a dry mouth and throat. Almost all users of marijuana report having the "munchies"—an increase in hunger after smoking the drug.

Marijuana does not have to be smoked in large quantities to increase physical and mental effects and the possibility of health problems for the user. Evidence suggests that small doses of marijuana can temporarily interfere with speech, memory, concentration, and

Symptoms and effects of marijuana depend largely on the strength of the drug, how it is used, and what the user expects will happen. However, almost all users report having the "munchies"—an increase in hunger after smoking marijuana.

learning. As a result, users can find it especially hard to learn and remember things. Dr. Alan I. Leshner is director of the National Institute on Drug Abuse (NIDA). He reported the results of a study showing that marijuana users had problems paying attention, learning, and remembering what they were taught. This was true even after they quit smoking the drug for a day. "All along, we've been telling young people not to smoke marijuana," said Dr. Leshner, "especially if they want to do well in school."[7]

One teen marijuana smoker was interviewed on a television news show. He explained marijuana's effects on him in this way: "It's so hard for me now to concentrate. Like someone will ask me a question, and I'll just have to ask them again because I will totally forget what they just said to me."[8] Researchers suggest that this problem could continue for some users even after they decide to give up marijuana for good.[9] Marijuana users have been known to have difficulty focusing on tasks such as reading, writing, swimming, and playing sports.

Teens who have smoked marijuana for a long time could find themselves becoming lazy. They may have little energy or willpower. Problems could include not caring what happens in their lives, tiredness, not caring about how they look, and having no desire to work or attend school.[10] Some find that marijuana increases their appetite. This could lead to gaining weight, which, although an undesirable effect for most teens, could actually benefit AIDS patients.

Problems Associated With Marijuana Use

In addition to dropping out of school, inability to make good choices or solve problems, and poor relationships

Marijuana users may have difficulty focusing on simple tasks such as reading, writing, or swimming.

with parents and friends, there are also tremendous expenses associated with using marijuana. One study was released in 1995 by the Center on Addiction and Substance Abuse at Columbia University. It revealed that the United States federal government spent more than $64 billion in health and disability care for people affected by drug abuse. More than one fourth of this amount was spent on marijuana users alone.[11] This amount includes treatment for marijuana smokers unable to quit on their own once they are hooked.

Marijuana and Public Safety

Marijuana is a threat to the millions who use it daily, but evidence suggests that the general public is at risk as well.

Marijuana has the power to intoxicate those behind the wheels of automobiles, buses, planes, boats, and other kinds of machinery. It poses a hazard to innocent people unaware that their lives could be in danger. There is very little reliable data available on this issue, but stories of mishaps have surfaced in the news.

On January 4, 1987, one of the worst railroad tragedies in American history occurred. An Amtrak passenger train collided with a Conrail train north of Washington, D.C. The aftermath was deadly. Sixteen passengers lost their lives and 175 were injured. Practically an entire train was destroyed. Investigators of the accident discovered that several of the engineers aboard the Conrail train had traces of marijuana in their system.[12]

Research has proven that personal and public safety is at risk any time someone is high or intoxicated from using mood-altering drugs.

Another accident involving marijuana seriously injured several members of the Detroit Red Wings hockey team on June 13, 1997. Police reported that the driver of the limousine in which three teammates were riding had marijuana in his blood when he crashed into a tree. Red Wings defenseman Vladimir Konstantinov and team masseur Sergei Mnatsakanov suffered severe head injuries. Another passenger, defenseman Slava Fetisov, sustained chest, lung, and knee injuries.[13]

Some marijuana smokers claim they are more careful driving a car or operating heavy machinery when under the influence of this drug. This is not the case, however. Research has proven that personal and public safety is at risk any time someone is high or intoxicated from using mood-changing drugs. And when alcohol is used with marijuana, the danger is considerably increased.

Marijuana and Crime

One important issue that continues to be debated is whether a connection exists between drug use and acts of violence or other crimes. In 1993 nearly 30 percent of male teens arrested in various cities had marijuana in their systems. More than half the young people arrested in Washington, D.C., in 1994 also tested positive for this drug.[14] This suggests that marijuana could possibly cause the user to commit a crime. Research has shown that criminals and drug users have much in common. Failing in school, broken families, and a lack of social skills are traits shared by both. Most criminals' lifestyles include involvement with illegal drugs.

Many arrests occur as a result of breaking the law while intoxicated on marijuana or other mood-altering and mind-altering drugs. Many other people face jail terms for crimes directly related to selling, possessing, or manufacturing drugs. The Federal Bureau of Investigation (FBI) reported that marijuana arrests for 1996 were the highest in American history. Nearly 589,000 youths and adults were charged with a marijuana crime. Some 85 percent of those arrests were for possession (not including sale or manufacture).[15] Fines and jail terms vary from state to state and can range from a few hundred dollars to thousands of dollars and several years in prison.

The consequences from smoking marijuana can be enormous. They can also be deadly. Consider the story of Julio Valerio, a sixteen-year-old boy from Phoenix,

Whether or not there is a direct connection between crime increases and marijuana use is still uncertain. However, research has shown that criminals and drug users have a great deal in common.

Arizona. He argued with his parents over smoking marijuana and left their home. A squabble with Phoenix police officers later proved fatal. After charging at officers with a butcher knife for no apparent reason, he was shot and killed instantly.[16] This tragedy was one that might have been avoided had Julio not been involved with marijuana, cocaine, methamphetamine, and alcohol.

Researchers still have much to explore about the relationship between marijuana and crime. While the answers are being sought, one thing is certain: Marijuana can alter behavior, causing the user to behave in unacceptable ways.

Robin (not her real name) is one teen who knows how marijuana use can change someone. After she went from smoking it once a month, to once a day, to all day long, her behavior and attitude changed.

> Pot wasn't making me mellow any more. I got to hating everybody, and I was violent all the time. For no reason at all I'd all of a sudden throw a violent tantrum, punching holes in the wall, scratching myself, pulling my hair out, screaming that I was going to kill myself.[17]

Eventually giving up marijuana after seeing its negative effects, Robin had help from her family, and she turned her life around by quitting the drug. She said, "I'm a totally different person now."[18]

Smoking marijuana can make users lose control, allowing the drug to rule their thoughts and actions. Robin was lucky she was able to see the way this drug made her act and was able to change before things became worse. Many teens never get this chance, and their lives are literally turned upside down.

three

Marijuana and Young Adults

Young people use marijuana for different reasons. Some kids and teens say they use marijuana because their friends do it, too. Some have brothers and sisters who smoke it. Others may think it looks cool. Many are just plain curious.

As different as these reasons seem, all of them have one thing in common. People smoke marijuana to change the way they feel: to feel better, to feel happy, to feel nothing, to forget, to be sociable, or to be accepted. Marijuana may seem like the best way to change a mood, take away pain, appear daring, or to be popular. Though the reasons may sound good, the results can often be bad.

Steven recalled how it was for him. At age thirteen he began smoking marijuana with a group of high school students. He explained what happened next:

One high [being under the influence of marijuana] led to another and still another. Somehow I never noticed that within a few months all my energies were centered on chasing weed. Every area of my life began to suffer, but I didn't care. I cut classes, began to lie to everyone, started running away from home when I didn't get my way, and eventually started stealing.[1]

Like many others, Steven wanted very much to be accepted. Sadly, his need to belong caused him more trouble than he expected.

People use marijuana because they think it will help them escape their problems. However, the effects rarely last long, and the problems that existed before smoking generally do not go away after smoking.

Marijuana has been known to get in the way of many

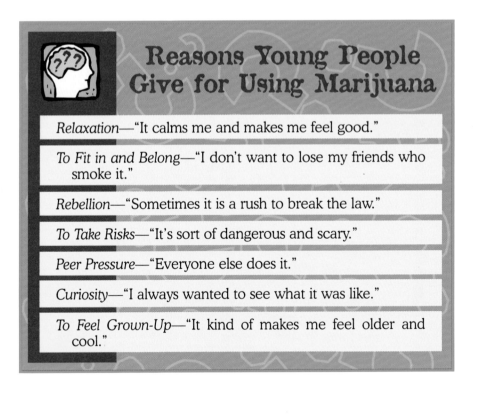

Reasons Young People Give for Using Marijuana

Relaxation—"It calms me and makes me feel good."

To Fit in and Belong—"I don't want to lose my friends who smoke it."

Rebellion—"Sometimes it is a rush to break the law."

To Take Risks—"It's sort of dangerous and scary."

Peer Pressure—"Everyone else does it."

Curiosity—"I always wanted to see what it was like."

To Feel Grown-Up—"It kind of makes me feel older and cool."

a young person's dreams and goals. Professional tennis player and Olympic gold medal-winner Jennifer Capriati is one of them. At thirteen years old she dazzled almost everyone on her first pro tour. Experts predicted she would soon be the best player ever. Her skills were near perfect, making her hard to beat.

Jennifer's dreams had come true. It had been her goal to become a tennis star. After a while, the pressure of being famous must have become intense. Surprising many in the sports world, she suddenly gave up tennis, quit school, and moved away from home.

Her life began to change. She was arrested for shoplifting, then for possessing a bag of marijuana. Rumors spread that she had been abusing other drugs as well. A close friend reported: "She has had a drug problem for at least a year."[2]

No matter how talented, intelligent, or popular a person is, marijuana and other drugs can lead to serious consequences. In February 1997 in Atlanta, Georgia, a car driven by eighteen-year-old Sanolay Nhavilay accidentally crashed into another car. The results were horrible. Nhavilay's sixteen-year-old friend, a passenger, died of severe head injuries. Police at the scene smelled a strong odor of marijuana in the car and on the driver. They charged Nhavilay with first-degree vehicular homicide and driving under the influence of this drug.[3]

An important rule to follow is to never get in a vehicle driven by someone who has taken drugs.

Helping a Friend

Most young people today know someone who uses marijuana or other drugs. They also have seen the harm it causes. A 1997 survey conducted by the Center on

Marijuana impairs a user's judgment. It is never wise to drive after smoking or to drive with someone who has smoked.

Addiction and Substance Abuse (CASA) found that high school students report that half of all of their friends use drugs every month. Some 52 percent of middle-school students say they know of someone who has been expelled or suspended from school for possessing, using, or selling drugs. In fact, 8 percent of thirteen-year-olds have classmates who have died because of drugs, including marijuana.[4]

A person does not have to be addicted to marijuana for it to cause problems. Even experimenting with it once or twice could lead to harm. There are clues, however, to look for to determine whether marijuana is beginning to take control of someone's life. Someone with one or more of the following signs may need help:

- avoiding friends who don't smoke marijuana;

- believing that smoking marijuana is the only way to have fun;

- feeling tired, run-down, depressed, or suicidal;

- getting into trouble with the law;

- getting suspended or dropping out of school;

- giving up activities that used to be fun, such as sports, reading, or music;

- lying about the amount of marijuana used;

- pressuring others to smoke marijuana;

- taking dangerous risks, including sexual risks; or

- talking all the time about getting high.

The effects from getting high can prevent users from thinking clearly enough to see the negative effects. This may be why it is so difficult to stop using marijuana.

It is possible to assist someone having difficulties as a result of marijuana use. The first step is to find out where help is available, should the person agree to it. Ask a parent, teacher, counselor, doctor, or minister for assistance. Next, express concern to the user about safety and the problems brought on by the drug. Do not criticize or condemn the user. Speak in a caring and kind way. Finally, suggest a person or a place the user can go to for help and support to quit the habit.

Helping Yourself

Marijuana users can answer the following questions to find out whether they have a problem with drug use.[5]

Answering yes to one or more of the following could indicate that a problem exists:

- Is it difficult to concentrate?
- Is it hard to remember things?
- Are personal appearance and hygiene being neglected?
- Is there a lack of motivation and self-esteem?
- Is there a loss of interest in activities, sports, and hobbies?
- Is there a drastic change in what is important?
- Have relationships with drug-taking friends become important?
- Have grades in school gone down?

Those who find they cannot quit smoking marijuana have to admit to a problem before they can get help. Sixteen-year-old Sara (not her real name) knows how hard this can be. She said: "I feel the most difficult problem I face as a sophomore is drugs," she said. "Now I'm not saying I'm a saint in this matter because I'm not, but it's just so hard to go a full day without cutting class to get high." Her advice for other teens is not to get involved with drugs in the first place. "If you do," she continued, "then try to stop, get help, and most of all—know that you are not alone. There are tons of people who would love to help you. You just have to let them."[6]

The resources listed in the "Where to Write for Help" section of this book can be a start.

four

Marijuana: What It Is and What It Does

There is still plenty to be learned about the effects of marijuana use over a long period. There is good reason, however, to believe it can be harmful. Because marijuana contains more than four hundred active ingredients, it is more difficult to study than other kinds of drugs. Many marijuana smokers consider it safe, but evidence suggests that it is more harmful than they think.

Marijuana was a slang term first used by soldiers in the Mexican-American War. It refers to a plant named *Cannabis sativa,* which means "useful hemp." Hemp is actually the stalks, stems, and roots of the marijuana plant. In the United States, only these parts of the plant are legal to possess and can be used for making clothing, paper, paints, plastics, cosmetics, and feed for animals.

Before the days of synthetic fabrics, both

George Washington and Thomas Jefferson grew crops of their own hemp. Many of the sails and ropes on colonial ships were made from hemp, as were Bibles and maps. In 1640, the governor of Connecticut declared that "every citizen must grow the plant," because it was badly needed for its fiber content.[1]

The flowers, buds, and leaves of the marijuana plant are all illegal. They are usually dried, crushed, and rolled into paper, like a cigarette. Sometimes marijuana is also smoked in a pipe or bong. Some people mix the drug into brownies or cookies for eating.

It is fairly easy to buy marijuana in the United States and Canada. The price ranges from forty to nine hundred

The flowers, buds, and leaves of the marijuana plant are usually dried, crushed, and rolled in paper, like a cigarette. Sometimes marijuana is also smoked in a pipe. Some people may also mix marijuana into brownies or cookie mix and bake it.

dollars an ounce, depending on the strength of the marijuana.[2] In the past decade, the cost of marijuana has dropped so low that most teenagers are able to afford it. It is one of the easiest illegal drugs to obtain.

Much of the marijuana used in the United States is grown in backyards, along river shores, hidden in cornfields, or sometimes indoors. Using special lights, high-grade soil, and expensive watering systems, growers are able to increase the potency of the drug. This increased potency makes it more desirable and more expensive.

In the United States most marijuana is grown in California, Hawaii, Kentucky, New York, Maine, Oregon, Tennessee, and Vermont. Much of it is secretly brought across the border from Mexico, however, shipments from Colombia and Jamaica are increasing.[3]

The marijuana plant has been grown for more than five thousand years. Ancient writings from China and India tell of it being used as medicine for pain, anxiety, and tension.[4] It was commonly brewed for drinking, much as tea is.

Over the years marijuana found its way into many other countries, including the United States and Canada. People used it for its hemp and to treat illnesses. They also used it for its pleasurable effects. As the drug became more popular, it spread from one end of the country to the other. By the 1930s marijuana was being sold on the streets in nearly every major city in the United States.[5] At that time, however, there were no laws against it.

Some government officials at the time saw marijuana as a dangerous drug. They had heard stories that it made people act crazy or go insane. There were tales of it

Mexican Marijuana Trafficking to U.S. States

WASHINGTON

CALIFORNIA

COLORADO

OKLAHOMA

MEXICO

TEXAS

LOUISIANA

Atlantic Ocean

Culiacan

Gulf of Mexico

Guadalajara

Pacific Ocean

Acapulco

A great deal of the marijuana that is found in the United States is secretly brought across the border from Mexico.

causing young people and adults to commit horrible crimes, including murder. An official from the Federal Bureau of Narcotics called marijuana "the Assassin of Youth," and he wanted it outlawed. Most of these stories were false, but many citizens and officials believed them and decided to make the drug illegal. They passed laws making it a Schedule I substance alongside other dangerous drugs.

Schedule I drugs are classified by government officials

as being dangerous, likely to cause harm, and lacking a perceived medical use.

Schedule II drugs have a high abuse potential with the possibility of severe physical dependence. They include amphetamine, cocaine, codeine, morphine, and opium. Schedule III drugs are considered less harmful than those in Schedules I and II. They include benphetanine, clortemine, and Tylenol^{TM} with codeine. Schedule IV drugs have even less potential for dependence and include barbital, chloral hydrate, and methohexital. Schedule V drugs are the least addictive and consist primarily of preparations containing limited quantities of certain narcotics and stimulants, such as buprenorphine and propylhexedine.

The new laws were meant to frighten marijuana users into giving up the drug, but that did not happen. Even with the threat of going to jail and paying expensive fines, many people continued smoking it.

Today, some states have lowered fines and jail time for those caught with marijuana. However, the laws can be tough, and many states send marijuana-using criminals to prison. Myths about marijuana continue

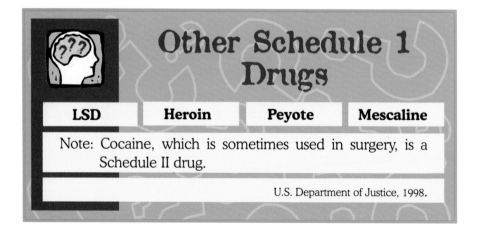

Other Schedule 1 Drugs

| LSD | Heroin | Peyote | Mescaline |

Note: Cocaine, which is sometimes used in surgery, is a Schedule II drug.

U.S. Department of Justice, 1998.

The Truth About Marijuana

Myths	Facts
Marijuana is safe because it is a natural plant.	Hundreds of natural plants can be unsafe and dangerous, including marijuana.
Smoking marijuana takes away stress.	Marijuana only temporarily eases stress and merely postpones having to deal with problems.
The use of marijuana does not lead to the use of other drugs.	Research shows that some marijuana users may be more at risk than others to start using dangerous drugs.
Marijuana wears off in an hour or two.	Because it is stored in the body's fatty cells, effects could be felt for weeks after use.
Alcohol is more dangerous than marijuana.	Like alcohol, marijuana is a dangerous substance that also contains cancer-causing chemicals.
Creative thoughts are brought on with marijuana use.	Marijuana clouds the mind and can interfere with speech, thinking, and memory.
Marijuana is safer today than it ever was before.	Today marijuana is more potent and dangerous than it ever was. Other drugs are sometimes mixed with it.

Source: Cathleen Shapley, "Marijuana: The Facts," Prevention Resources, Inc., 1997, p. 2.

today. Some people argue that because it is a naturally grown plant, it is harmless. Though some people claim it has helped them with certain illnesses, there is proof that it can also be dangerous. Any drug or plant that changes the way the brain works can cause physical and emotional problems.

The Physical Effects of Marijuana

Marijuana contains more than four hundred dangerous chemicals. One of the best known of these chemicals is THC (delta-9-tetrahydrocannabinol). This is the main chemical in marijuana that changes how the brain works. The amount of THC in the marijuana helps determine how strong its effects may be. The type of plant, the weather, the soil, and other factors determine the strength. Within seconds of smoking marijuana, its chemicals enter the lungs. From there, they go into the bloodstream. In minutes they enter the brain, making the user feel high, or stoned. This can sometimes last any where from ten minutes to four hours. Once it begins to wear off, the user generally feels tired, hungry, and somewhat depressed. This is called a marijuana hangover.

In heavy users of marijuana, traces of THC can sometimes stay in their system for several weeks after they have stopped using the drug. Teens who smoke marijuana nearly every day never rid their body of it unless they quit. Marijuana stays in the body because THC is fat soluble, meaning it stores itself in the body's fat cells.[6] Fatty areas such as the brain, liver, kidneys, lungs, testicles, and ovaries can be greatly affected by this chemical. It remains in these areas for long periods before leaving the body. Scientists continue to study how marijuana affects the health of those who use it. So far they believe it can cause problems in various areas of the body.

Lungs

Researchers believe marijuana can be especially harmful to the lungs. Users often inhale the harsh, unfiltered

THC is the main chemical found in marijuana. The amount of THC in marijuana helps determine how strong the drug's effects may be.

smoke deeply and hold it in as long as possible before letting it out. Because the smoke is in contact with lung tissue for a long time, it irritates and eventually damages the lungs.

The smoke from marijuana contains some of the same chemicals that are found in tobacco smoke. These chemicals cause sore throats and coughs; they can also lead to bronchitis and the lung disease emphysema, as well as cancer. In addition, many people who smoke marijuana also smoke store-bought tobacco cigarettes. The effects of combining these two substances could lead to added health problems.[7]

Scientists at the University of California, Los Angeles,

discovered that smoking one to three marijuana joints a day is as dangerous and health-threatening as smoking fifteen tobacco cigarettes—almost an entire pack.[8]

Heart

A single marijuana joint causes the heart to work faster. Almost immediately after smoking it, the heart rate increases as much as 50 percent. This can also make blood pressure rise.[9] For those who already have high blood pressure or heart problems, smoking marijuana could cause serious health risks.

Brain

It is not clear whether marijuana permanently damages the brain. In 1972, however, one study in England reported evidence of two marijuana smokers whose brains had been severely damaged by the drug.[10]

It is certain that marijuana affects nerve cells in the part of the brain where memories are formed. As a result, marijuana users have a difficult time remembering important facts. Scientists are still trying to figure out whether this might lead to permanent memory loss.[11]

Any drug, whether illegal or prescribed by a doctor, that changes the chemistry of the brain, can be dangerous, according to researchers. And because THC stays in the fatty cells of the brain longer than any other drug, it could be especially harmful.

Reproduction

The reproductive cells in both males and females are high in fat, and they absorb more THC than most other organs. This THC absorption can cause sperm reduction in men and interfere with menstrual cycles in women.[12] Even worse, marijuana could possibly damage the supply of eggs in the ovaries.[13] If this were to happen, the user could never have children.

Immune System

A healthy immune system is important. It protects us by fighting off infections and disease. Scientists have learned that marijuana smokers are less immune to certain health problems than are nonsmokers. This is because the drug stops white blood cells from growing.[14] White blood cells are important in protecting people from getting sick.

In 1995 alone, more than forty-seven thousand people were treated at emergency rooms across the United States for marijuana-related illnesses.[15] Most were for some of the side effects brought on by using marijuana. Severe anxiety, paranoia, and panic attacks were the most common. Some users had been involved

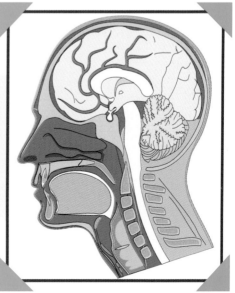

Marijuana has been proven to affect nerve cells in the part of the brain where memories are formed. As a result, marijuana users often have trouble remembering important facts.

Thousands of people end up in hospital emergency rooms each year as a result of marijuana-related illnesses.

in accidents, including automobile crashes, while driving under the influence of this drug. This can be especially dangerous. Marijuana can interfere with driving skills for at least four to six hours after smoking a single cigarette.[16]

Besides these health problems, marijuana has also been linked to risk-taking behaviors that could factor into the increase in the spread of sexually transmitted diseases, including HIV-AIDS. Most drugs that alter a person's mood, including marijuana, can make it hard to think clearly. This can cause users to go against their values and morals and make choices they might otherwise avoid.

Addiction

Not everyone who uses marijuana becomes addicted. Those who do, usually find themselves using the drug more and more often. It becomes difficult to quit and becomes a big part of their daily life. This effect is known as tolerance. No one ever expects to get hooked. The user is usually the last to realize it. Most people become aware of their addiction after they have had many problems in their life caused by their addiction or use of drugs.

Heather (not her real name) is a good example. Her grades in high school dropped from an A average to a D average. She began missing class and gave up many of her school activities. She felt sick most the time. She lost her drive and motivation. Smoking marijuana became a big part of her life. Even with all the problems it caused, it was difficult to quit.

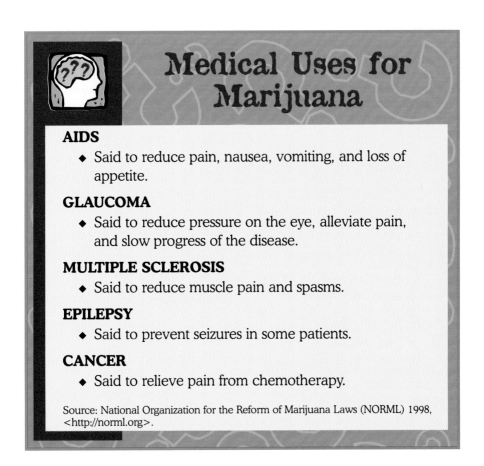

Medical Uses for Marijuana

AIDS
- ◆ Said to reduce pain, nausea, vomiting, and loss of appetite.

GLAUCOMA
- ◆ Said to reduce pressure on the eye, alleviate pain, and slow progress of the disease.

MULTIPLE SCLEROSIS
- ◆ Said to reduce muscle pain and spasms.

EPILEPSY
- ◆ Said to prevent seizures in some patients.

CANCER
- ◆ Said to relieve pain from chemotherapy.

Source: National Organization for the Reform of Marijuana Laws (NORML) 1998, <http://norml.org>.

Writing in her journal, Heather described her addiction this way: "Pot is a motionless sea of destruction. I'm drowning."[17] Getting hooked on marijuana can happen to anyone at anytime. There is no way of telling who could be next. Researchers also suggest that marijuana smokers stand a greater risk of trying even more dangerous drugs. This risk has earned marijuana its reputation as a "gateway" drug. Along with alcohol and tobacco, it has been blamed as one of the first drugs most people use before moving on to more dangerous ones.

Marijuana smokers between the ages of twelve and seventeen are eighty-five times more likely to try cocaine than are nonsmokers.[18] It appears that the best way to protect against having a drug problem is to not use any of them at all.

Marijuana as Medicine

Though marijuana can cause problems, advocates say it can also assist people with certain illnesses. In 1996 voters in California and Arizona passed laws making marijuana legal for health purposes. Under these laws, marijuana can be used only if a doctor recommends it.

five

Prevention and Treatment

Some drug prevention programs in the United States are offered through the schools. Most are presented by law enforcement agencies, health professionals, and community action centers. Though all are different in many ways, they still have one goal in common—preventing young people from ever getting started on marijuana.

What seems to work best in most of these programs is encouraging young people to find better things to do than smoke marijuana. Involvement in sports, the arts, and hobbies are a just a few of the alternatives taught. Dr. Lloyd Johnston is a researcher at the University of Michigan. He had this to say of teens, during a National Marijuana Conference in 1995: "They have to learn why they shouldn't do drugs because they live in an environment where drugs are all around them. They have to have a reason not to use drugs. Someone has to teach them."[1]

School Programs

Most students reaching the twelfth grade have been educated about the risks associated with marijuana abuse. It may have been taught by a health teacher, police officer, or school counselor. Drug prevention programs provide more than simply instructing students to "just say no."

One highly successful program is at the high school in Palatine, Illinois. More than 70 percent of the students there are involved in sports or other healthy activities. Before they are allowed to participate, they each must sign a "code of conduct," promising to remain drug-free. Athletes and their parents are also required to attend meetings to learn valuable information about marijuana and other drugs.

All the athletes wear T-shirts each Friday, proclaiming "Drug-Free Athlete." Principal Nancy Robb said, "These are high profile kids who serve as terrific role models for others."[2] This had had a real impact. Many of the high school students are learning that it is not cool to smoke marijuana or use other drugs.

Some young children are learning about the dangers of drugs even before they enter kindergarten. In Texas, preschoolers are taught the difference between useful medications and harmful street drugs.[3] Program organizers hope that these children will remember what they learned and make the choice not to use marijuana and other illegal drugs as they get older. Drug prevention experts say that the younger a child learns about the dangers of different drugs, the lower the risk is of that child ever becoming involved with drugs as he or she grows up.

There are many rewarding activities, such as team sports, in which students can participate—without having to rely on drugs to make them feel good.

Community Programs

Communities have sponsored drug prevention programs for years. They were used mainly to teach parents how to raise drug-free children. That focus has changed, and programs are now beginning to appreciate the importance of involving young people.

"Halfway There" is a powerful program made up entirely of teens. These young people use drama to act out their past experiences with drugs. They travel across the United States and perform for hundreds of thousands of young people and their parents. The skits they put on reflect what can happen to young people who make poor choices. They also show the positive alternatives to drugs.

One student observed that "the actors and actresses were so real-to-life that it was scary."[4] However, the show is also filled with music, humor, and hope. It makes a lasting impression on all who see it.

Prevention programs do not work well for young people already using marijuana. This is especially true if they are hooked. If this is the case, intervention and a treatment program may be needed.

"I tried quitting on my own and found it wasn't as easy a I had thought," explained David (not his real name), a fourteen-year-old ex-marijuana smoker. "That's when my mom and dad suggested I check into a place that could help. It worked. I haven't used pot since getting out."[5]

Treatment Programs

Marijuana addiction has harmed the lives of thousands of young people. It is not an easy illness to treat. No treatment program will succeed unless the person admits to a marijuana problem and accepts the help offered. Each program is different and depends on the severity of the addiction.

Inpatient Treatment

Inpatient programs provide education and counseling in a hospital or rehabilitation center. They provide a safe place away from old drug-using friends and other dangerous situations. Patients focus more on their lives and learn valuable skills to help them stay away from marijuana in the future. Inpatient programs usually last a month or two, and they can cost as much as twenty-five thousand dollars. This is about the same as one year of college at many universities today.

Residential Treatment

Teens unable or unwilling to stay off marijuana or other drugs after attending inpatient treatment are usually sent to residential treatment centers. Programs of this type are long-term, lasting from twelve to eighteen months. Some of these programs are set in the wilderness. An exciting one is the Selkirk Healing Center in Manitoba, Canada. Here, teens learn valuable spiritual lessons from American Indians.[6]

Ceremonial dances, healing circles, and powwows are some of the daily activities. Patients are able to gain a better understanding of themselves and gain greater confidence. This program has helped many young people to give up drugs and become better citizens by raising their self-esteem, making them feel better about themselves, and teaching them skills to be more able to achieve their goals.

Outpatient Treatment

Outpatient treatment is considered a less intense treatment. Patients attend one to five counseling groups a week for up to a year. They are able to live at home, attend school, work, and continue receiving the help they need.

Most teens who have completed a program in an inpatient or residential setting are referred to this type of treatment for additional moral support and prevention education. It's almost like a safety net in case they get any urges to begin smoking marijuana again.

Prevention and treatment programs are important ways of teaching young people skills to easily refuse marijuana and remain drug-free. Most require staying away from one of the most powerful influences there is— peer pressure. Kim, a young woman who finally gave up drugs, realized this. "At one time," she said, "these people [drug-using friends] meant more to me than I meant to myself. But that got me nowhere."[7] Taking charge of one's own life and becoming a leader instead of a follower is the simplest way to avoid being tempted to smoke marijuana.

Support Groups

Nearly all treatment programs recommend attending support meetings one or more times a week. They have been proven helpful in remaining clean and sober from marijuana and other types of drugs. These meetings are free, and are held in thousands of cities across the United States and Canada. Some can even be found in Russia, Germany, and England.

Support groups are made up entirely of people recovering from drugs. They are anonymous, and no one is supposed to mention whom they see there. Members discuss how drugs have affected their lives and the various things they have done to quit. Each person is there to offer support and guidance to one another.

Marijuana Anonymous is the main support group for those addicted to marijuana. The only requirement for membership is a desire to stop using the drug. Some meetings have guest speakers. Others might read literature about recovery. Many meetings have a topic for discussion. When Mark (not his real name) went to his first Marijuana Anonymous meeting, he described it as an "incredible experience." He went on to say:

> I knew I had a problem by that time, but I never really considered myself a marijuana addict. After all, it was "only pot," a lie I had been repeating to myself for years. I heard other recovering addicts share their experiences.

When they talked about not liking themselves and loving pot more than anything else, I identified completely. I had lived through just what these people were talking about: the lies, the self pity, the continual blaming of others, the refusal to take personal responsibility for my own life. These were things I was convinced only I had experienced.

I heard something else in that meeting, however, that made a profound impact on my life—I heard people share their hope and strength as recovering addicts. I saw for the first time that it was possible to live without smoking pot. All I needed was honesty, open-mindedness, and willingness.[8]

The purpose of attending support groups on a regular basis is to make friends and learn to have fun again

Many students in schools across the country have made a promise to remain drug-free. The marijuana plants being burned here are a reminder that it is not cool to smoke marijuana or use other illegal drugs.

without having to depend on a drug to do this. These groups help millions of people every day to discover life without the use of marijuana or other drugs. Joy (not her real name), a fifteen-year-old recovering addict, explained it in this way:

> I used to think that only the kids who got high were cool, but now I find that these kids bore me. The kids who don't get high have more to say, do more things, and are a lot more fun to be around. I have made many friends with them. Nobody likes a drooping dopehead, except other drooping dopeheads.[9]

Besides Marijuana Anonymous, there are other types of support groups that are also helpful to recovering teens and adults. A popular one is Narcotics Anonymous. It is intended for people addicted to other kinds of drugs besides just marijuana. Another program is Alcoholics Anonymous. It is primarily for people having a problem with alcohol, yet it accepts those addicted to other drugs as well, Marijuana Anonymous, Alcoholics Anonymous, and Narcotics Anonymous all profess the same motto:

> *Grant me the serenity to accept the things I cannot change; courage to change the things I can; and the wisdom to know the difference.*

six

Peer Pressure

Peer pressure is a fact of life. It can make people do things they do not really want to do. As young people get older, they usually find themselves pressured more and more by friends. It is the fear of being seen as different or being shunned that causes most people to do what others are doing—even when it could be wrong.

Ellen was a teenager who moved with her parents to a new town. Wanting to find friends and fit in, she was afraid to talk about her goals and interests in science, technology, and going to college. She went so far as checking out books on these subjects at the public library instead of at her school. Ellen did not want anyone to think of her as a "nerd" or "brain."

She even pretended to sleep during classes that interested her to make other students think she was "cool" and "one of them." "I pretended my only interest in life was getting high," she recalled. Her real purpose was to get attention and be popular.

Though she was against drugs, Ellen hung out with those teens who were known to be stoned most of the time. Eventually she began doing the same. It was not long before she was getting in trouble with teachers and some of the students that were drug-free. Her world of friends became smaller and smaller. Finally Ellen discovered that she didn't have a single true friend. Her drug-using friends were more interested in themselves and staying high than in her and who she really was. "Drugs had given me the illusion of having friends, but they couldn't give me the real thing," she said. "In fact, they prevented me from making friends with the kind of people who shared my interest in science. After all, future doctors and engineers had better things to do with their time than watch me fry my brains."[1]

Once Ellen was ready to give up drugs, she started working toward her goals without worrying about what others would think. For many people who continue worrying about what others might think, their problems can become far worse. They might include arrests, accidents, and addiction.

The easiest ways to avoid pressure to smoke marijuana are

- avoiding places where marijuana and other drugs are available;
- being involved in community activities or volunteer work;
- finding friends who do not use it;
- learning a relaxing craft, such as quilting, woodworking, ceramics, or painting;

True friends (like the ones shown here) would never encourage or participate in drug use.

- ◆ speaking out against and educating others about the dangers of marijuana;
- ◆ staying happy and healthy by exercising or playing sports; and
- ◆ taking personal pride in living life drug-free.

Skills for Drug-Free Living

It is impossible to predict who will and who will not experiment with marijuana at sometime. It has been proven, however, that the more involved a person is in something safe, positive, and exciting, the less likely that person will be to try the drug or to abuse it.

One counselor who works with marijuana-addicted

youth noted, "Kids we see in treatment lack many of the skills needed to keep from being bored or depressed. They begin looking for a fast and simpler way to feel better like smoking pot." She went on to say, "We rarely see kids that are involved in healthy activities, such as 4-H clubs, scouting, sports, or those learning new things like dancing or playing a musical instrument."[2]

Regardless of what many marijuana smokers say, the majority of young people shy away from this drug. In fact, more than 70 percent of eighth graders strongly disapproved of people who have tried marijuana once or even twice. Close to 80 percent disapproved of its' being smoked occasionally. Over 85 percent disapproved of its' being used on a regular basis.[3]

What happens when the pressure is too much to handle, even for people who are strongly against smoking marijuana? How can they safely get out of a situation where a marijuana joint is suddenly handed to them? Here are some steps that may help:

Ask Questions. If unknown substances are offered, ask, "What is it?" and "Where did you get it?"

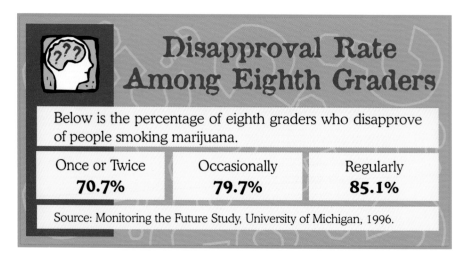

Disapproval Rate Among Eighth Graders

Below is the percentage of eighth graders who disapprove of people smoking marijuana.

Once or Twice	Occasionally	Regularly
70.7%	**79.7%**	**85.1%**

Source: Monitoring the Future Study, University of Michigan, 1996.

Give reasons. "My parents will kill me" or "The coach says drugs will hurt my game" are examples of some reasons that young people use.

Suggest other things to do. If a friend is offering marijuana, just saying no is tough and may not work well. Suggest doing something else—going to a movie, or working together on a school project. This strategy shows that the marijuana is being rejected, not the friend.

Leave. When all these steps have been tried, get out of the situation immediately. Go home, go to class, join a group of drug-free friends, or talk to someone else.[4]

"The best protection to keep from being pushed into trying marijuana is to stay away from those who smoke it," said thirteen-year-old Brandy (not her real name.) "I try and make sure my friends are drug-free. This way I don't have to worry so much about peer pressure and all the trouble it can cause."[5]

Healthy Choices

World figure-skating champion Tonia Kwiatkowski knows all about the benefits of staying drug-free. She said,

> Who cares what other people think? You have to look at what's best for you and what's best for your body. Being an athlete, I know that drugs and alcohol are not best for me. The most important thing is to feel comfortable with your decision, and be confident in your choices.[6]

Young people should never be afraid to stand up for what they believe in. As fifteen-year-old Tricia from California said: "You can't please everybody, so please yourself, be an individual."[7] There are millions of young people who choose not to use.

questions
for discussion

1. What do you think should be done to stop young people from using marijuana?
2. What would you do if you found out your best friend was a daily marijuana user?
3. If you were pressured by friends to smoke marijuana, what would you do? What would you say?
4. Why do think it is so difficult to keep people from using marijuana?
5. The United States and Canada have tried for years to educate citizens about the harmful effects of marijuana. Do you believe they are doing a good or a poor job at it?
6. If you discovered you had a problem with marijuana abuse and wanted to quit, who would you turn to for help?
7. How do you feel about teenagers who wear hats and T-shirts showing pictures of marijuana leaves?
8. Do you consider marijuana a safe or a dangerous drug?
9. If you were faced with a stressful situation that was difficult to solve, how would you cope without turning to marijuana?
10. Do you think marijuana is a big problem in your school? If so, what can be done about it?

chapter notes

Chapter 1. Shannon's Story

1. Author interview with "Shannon," September 21, 1997.

Chapter 2. Marijuana and Society

1. U.S. Department of Health and Human Services, *Tips for Teens About Marijuana* (Washington, D.C.: U.S. Department of Health and Human Services, 1995), p. 2.

2. National Parent's Resource Institute for Drug Education Survey, Atlanta 1997.

3. Joseph Gfoerer, *Preliminary Estimates from the 1995 National Household Survey on Drug Abuse: Advance Report Number 18* (Rockville, Md.: Substance Abuse and Mental Health Services Administration, August 1996), pp. 26–27.

4. National Institutes of Health, *Marijuana: Facts Parents Need to Know* (Bethesda, Md.: National Institutes of Health, 1995), pp. 1–2.

5. Center for Substance Abuse Prevention, *Prevention Primer: An Encyclopedia of Alcohol, Tobacco, and Other Drug Prevention Terms* (Rockville, Md.: National Clearinghouse for Alcohol and Drug Information, 1994), pp. 7–8.

6. Richard Fields, *Drugs in Perspective*, 2nd. ed. (Madison, Wis.: Brown and Benchmark Publishers, 1995), p. 251.

7. National Institute on Drug Abuse, press release, February 20, 1996, p. 1.

8. "Junior High," ABC *Primetime Live*, March 19, 1997.

9. National Institute on Drug Abuse, press release, February 20, 1996.

10. *Marijuana: Facts Parents Need to Know*, p. 22.

11. "The Tragedy of Marijuana," Columbia University Record, vol. 20, no. 19, March 3, 1995.

12. "Engineers in Amtrak Crash Guilty of Manslaughter in Plea Bargain," *The New York Times*, February 17, 1988, p. A-10.

13. Mike Nadel, "The Vladinator," *Los Angeles Times*, August 3, 1997, sports section, p. 1.

14. Daniel R. Levine, "Drugs Are Back—Big Time," *Reader's Digest*, February 1996, p. 76.

15. *Crime in the United States* (Washington, D.C.: FBI Uniform Code Reports, 1995), p. 54.

16. Jim Walsh, *The Arizona Republic*, December 21, 1996, Arizona Central Online Community, Phoenix Newspapers, Inc., "16-Year-Old Shot by Police," <http://www.acentral.com/> November 2, 1998.

17. Glenn Alan Cheney, *Drugs, Teens, and Recovery: Real-Life Stories of Trying to Stay Clean* (Hillside, N.J.: Enslow Publishers, Inc., 1993), pp. 47–48.

18. Ibid., p. 53.

Chapter 3. Marijuana and Young Adults

1. Steven Hurd, "My Story: What Drugs Can Do for Your Life," *Listen*, March 1997, p. 14.

2. Susan Reed, "Losing Her Grip: A Teen Star's Arrest Raises Hard Questions About How Fast a Gifted Child Can Be Pushed," *People*, May 30, 1994, p. 82.

3. Bill Montgomery, "Police Blotter: Driver Charged in Teen's Death," *The Atlanta Journal and Constitution*, February 27, 1997, electronic library, <http://www.elibrary.com/>.

4. "Back to School Survey 1997 Press Release," Center on Addiction and Substance Abuse, September, 8, 1997.

5. Gary L. Somdahl, *Drugs and Kids: How Parents Can Keep Them Apart* (Salem, Oreg.: Dimi Press, 1996), pp. 71–78.

6. Gayle Kimball, *The Teen Trip: The Complete Resource Guide*, (Chico, Calif.: Equality Press, 1997), p. 166.

Chapter 4. Marijuana: What It Is and What It Does

1. "About Hemp," National Organization for the Reform of Marijuana Laws, n.d., <http://www.netnorml.org/facts/hemp.html>, June 26, 1998.

2. "The NNICC Report 1995: The Supply of Illicit Drugs to the United States," National Narcotics Intelligence Consumers Committee, 1995.

3. "About Hemp," <http://www.netnorml.org/facts/hemp.html>.

4. Dorothy E. Dusek and Daniel A. Girdano, *Drugs: A Factual Account*, 4th ed. (New York: Random House, 1987), p. 95.

5. Ernest I. Abel, "Marijuana," Colliers Encyclopedia CD-ROM, February 28, 1996.

6. Anthony Radcliffe, Peter Rush, Carol Foffor Sites, Joe Cruse, "The Pharmer's Almanac: Pharmacology of Drugs," Mac Publishing, 1990, p. 129.

7. *Marijuana* (Rockville, Md.: National Institute on Drug Abuse, 1996), p. 4.

8. *Marijuana Update Capsule #12* (Rockville, Md.: National Institute on Drug Abuse, May 1996), p. 2.

9. W. R. Spence, *Marijuana: How Much of a Gamble?* (Waco, Tex.: Health Edco, Inc., 1987), p. 11.

10. Oakley S. Ray and Charles Ksir, Ph.D., *Drugs, Society, and the Human Behavior*, 7th ed. (St. Louis: Mosby-Yearbook, Inc., 1996), p. 421.

11. David P. Friedman, *Drugs and the Brain* (Bethesda, Md.: National Institutes of Health, April 1993), p. 12.

12. Brent Q. Hafen and David Soulier, *Marijuana: Facts, Figures, and Information* (Center City, Minn.: Hazelden Publishing Group, 1989), p. 31.

13. Spence, p. 13.

14. "How Marijuana May Affect Immunity," *Science News*, July 18, 1997, p. 46.

15. "Drug Abuse Warning Network Report," (DAWN), 1995.

16. *Prevention Plus II: Tools for Creating and Sustaining Drug-Free Communities* (Washington, D.C.: Office for Substance Abuse Prevention, 1989), p. 365.

17. Per Ola and Emily D'Aulaire, "But It's Only Pot," *Reader's Digest*, January 1997, p. 86.

18. Daniel R. Levine, "Drugs Are Back—Big Time," *Reader's Digest*, February 1996, p. 76.

Chapter 5. Prevention and Treatment

1. "Marijuana: A Recurring Problem," The Prevention Pipeline, National Clearinghouse for Alcohol and Drug Information (NCADI), September/October 1995, <http://www.health.org/>, November 2, 1998.

2. *Success Stories from Drug-Free Schools* (Washington, D.C.: U.S. Department of Education, 1992), p. 11.

3. Ibid., p. 31

4. *Halfway There: A Powerful Drama for Drug Abuse Prevention* (Detroit, Mich.: Halfway There, Inc., 1997), p. 1.

5. Author interview with "David," October 2, 1997.

6. "The Selkirk Healing Center: A Non-Profit Registered Charitable Organization," pamphlet (Manitoba, Canada: Leaf, Inc., 1997), p. 1.

7. Shelly Marshall, *Young, Sober, and Free* (Center City, Minn.: Hazelden Publishing Group, 1978), p. 53.

8. Author Interview with "Mark," September 29, 1997.

9. Marshall, p. 70.

Chapter 6. Peer Pressure

1. Ellen Harley, "How I Learned That Drugs Are No Way to Make Friends," *Listen*, August, 1986, pp. 24–25.

2. Author interview with "Cathy," October 6, 1997.

3. "The Monitoring the Future Study: 1996," University of Michigan, 1996.

4. *Growing Up Drug-Free: A Parent's Guide to Drug Prevention* (Washington, D.C.: U.S. Department of Education, 1995), p. 13.

5. Author interview with "Brandy," December 23, 1997

6. Alina Sivorinovsky, "The Heart of a Winner," *Listen*, January 1997, p. 19.

7. Gayle Kimball, Ph.D., *The Teen Trip: The Complete Resource Guide* (Chico, Calif.: Equality Press, 1997), p. 126.

where to write for help

American Council for Drug Education
164 West 74th St.
New York, NY 10023
(800) 488-3784
<http://www.acde.org/>

Canadian Centre on Substance Abuse
75 Albert St., Suite 300
Ottawa, ON Canada KIP 5E7
(613) 235-4048
<http://www.ccsa.ca/default.htm>

Join Together
441 Stuart St., 6th Floor
Boston, MA 02116
(617) 437-1500
<http://www.jointogether.org/jto/>

Marijuana Anonymous World Services
P.O. Box 2912
Van Nuys, CA 91404
(800) 766-6779
<http://marijuana-anonymous.org/>

Narcotics Anonymous
11426 Rockville Pike, Suite 100
Rockville, MD 20852
(301) 468-0985
<http://www.wsoinc.com/index.htm>

**National Clearinghouse for Alcohol
and Drug Information**
P.O. Box 2345
Rockville, MD 20847
(800) 729-6686
<http://www.health.org/>

National Families in Action
Century Plaza II
2957 Clairmont Road, Suite 150
Atlanta, GA 30329
(404) 248-9676
<http://www.emory.edu/NFIA/>

National Institute on Drug Abuse
5600 Fishers Lane, Room 10A03
Rockville, MD 20857
(301) 443-4577
<http://www.nida.nih.gov/>

Parent's Resource Institute for Drug Education
3610 DeKalb Technology Pkwy., Suite 105
Atlanta, GA 30340
(800) 853-7867
<http://www.prideusa.org/main.htm>

Partnership for a Drug-Free America
405 Lexington Ave., Suite 1601
New York, NY 10174
(212) 922-1560
<http://www.drugfreeamerica.org/index.html>

further reading

Berger, Gilda. *Meg's Story: Straight Talk About Drugs.* Brookfield, Conn.: Milbrook Press, 1994.

Cheney, Alan Glenn. *Drugs, Teens and Recovery: Real-Life Stories of Trying to Stay Clean.* Hillside, NJ: Enslow Publishers Inc., 1993.

Chier, Ruth. *Danger: Marijuana.* New York: Rosen Publishing Group, 1996.

McLaughlin, Miriam, and Hazouri Sandra Peyser. *Addiction: The "High" That Brings You Down.* Springfield, N.J.: Enslow Publishers Inc., 1997.

Mooney, Al, Arlene Eisenberg, and Howard Eisenberg. *The Recovery Book.* New York: Workman Publishing Company Inc., 1992.

Roos, Stephen. *A Young Person's Guide to the Twelve Steps.* Center City, Minn.: Hazelden Publishing Group, 1993.

Scott, Sharon. *How to Say No and Keep Your Friends: Peer Pressure Reversal for Teens and Preteens.* Amherst, Mass.: Human Resource Development Press, 1997.

Scott, Sharon, and George Phillips. *Too Cool for Drugs.* Amherst, Mass.: Human Resource Development Press, 1997.

Internet Addresses

National Institute on Drug Abuse (NIDA)
<http://www.nida.nih.gov/NIDAHome.html>

Marijuana Special Report: Addiction, Safety, Effects on Your Brain
<http://marijuana.newscientist.com/>

index